A Witch's Joke Book

Wilhelmina Woods

To all the witches out there who've ever accidentally turned a cake into a cauldron explosion or brewed a potion that was too bubbly.
May your brooms always fly straight, your cauldrons never overflow, and your cookies never turn into frogs... again!

Book Cover by Tukotuku Publishing

Illustrations by Tukotuku Publishing

First edition 2024

Print   978-1-991306-41-8

Ebook   978-1-991306-42-5

Contents

The Giggling Cauldron

Welcome to the most magical joke book in the witching world! Inside, you'll find more laughter than a witch's cackle and more magical mishaps than you can shake a broomstick at. Prepare to meet witches who can't quite keep their broomsticks straight, potions that bubble over with silliness, and spellbooks that seem to have a mind of their own. So grab your wand (or maybe just a snack), and get ready for a spellbindingly funny adventure! Just remember: no vanishing spells on the punchlines!

The Witch's Wardrobe

Witches aren't just about brewing potions and casting spells—they've got serious style too! Whether it's pointy hats, flowing robes, or broomstick accessories, witches know how to make a fashion statement. So, let's step into the magical closet and discover some hilarious jokes about witches' wardrobes!

Why do witches wear pointy hats?

- Because they always want to look sharp!

Why did the witch refuse to wear a cloak?

- She didn't want to look *cloak-y*.

What's a witch's favorite accessory for her broomstick?

- A handlebar mustache!

Why did the witch wear mismatched socks?

- Because she wanted to keep her magic *un-paired*!

Why don't witches wear flip-flops?

- They're afraid of toe spells!

Why did the witch buy a striped robe?

- She wanted to stand out in *spell-bound* fashion!

What do witches use to hang their clothes?

- *Spell-ders*!

Why did the witch wear a belt?

- To keep her wardrobe from *unraveling*!

What did the witch say when her hat flew off in the wind?

- "Well, that's just *hat-trocious*!"

Why don't witches wear high heels?

- Because they don't want to *trip up* their magic.

What's a witch's favorite kind of shoe?

- *Sneak-ers*—so they can sneak up on their spells!

What do you call a witch in pajamas?

- *Sleepy-head* witch!

Why do witches love pockets in their robes?

- So they can carry extra spells and snacks, of course!

Why do witches never wear suits?

- They prefer to dress down for a casual *spell*.

What do witches wear when it's cold?

- Their *spell-ter coats*.

Why did the witch wear a sparkly scarf?

- To *wrap up* her look with some magic!

What do you call a witch with too many hats?

- A *hat-hoarder*!

Why don't witches wear polka dots?

- Because they don't want to look like they've been *spot-ted*.

What happened when the witch lost her favorite cloak?

- She had to get a *cloak and dagger* to find it!

Why did the witch wear neon robes?

- So she could glow in the *dark arts*!

Why did the witch wear glasses?

- To help her see her *witchcraft* more clearly!

What's a witch's favorite piece of jewelry?

- A charm bracelet—literally filled with magical charms!

Why don't witches wear swimsuits?

- Because they don't want their magic to *dry up*.

What did the witch say when her robe didn't fit?

- "Looks like I'll need to *alter* it with a spell!"

Why did the witch wear a scarf in summer?

- To keep her *magic cool*!

What's a witch's favorite fashion magazine?

- *Vogue-spell*!

Why did the witch wear a tutu?

- Because she thought it was *spell-tacular*!

What do witches use to keep their hats from falling off?

- *Hat-pins*—enchanted, of course!

Why don't witches wear sunglasses?

- Because their magic shines too brightly already!

Why did the witch wear a polka-dotted dress?

- To show off her *spot-on* style!

What's a witch's favorite clothing store?

- *Hocus Pocus* Fashion Emporium!

Why do witches always look great in black?

- It's slimming and perfect for *casting shadows*.

What did the witch say about her glittery robe?

- "It's my *glamour spell*!"

Why don't witches wear leather?

- Because they'd rather wear *cloak* than *croak*.

What's a witch's favorite hat shop?

- The *Hocus Hat-us*!

What do witches wear when it rains?

- Their *witcherproof* cloaks!

Why did the witch love wearing high boots?

- So she could keep her *magic up to her knees*!

What did the witch say when she spilled potion on her robe?

- "Well, this is *cloak-tastrophe*!"

What does a witch use to polish her shoes?

- *Spell-shine*!

Why do witches always wear black boots?

- Because they go with everything—including *broomsticks*.

What kind of coat does a witch wear in the snow?

- A *witch-hiker* jacket!

Why did the witch wear rainbow-colored shoes?

- To keep her steps *spell-bright*!

What do witches wear at the beach?

- *Sand-witch* shoes!

Why did the witch wear a polka-dot hat?

- She thought it would help her *spot* more magical opportunities!

What do witches wear when they're feeling fancy?

- *Cloak-tails*!

What do witches call their comfy clothes?

- Their *witch-wear*.

Why did the witch wear purple shoes?

- To match her magical *violet spells*!

What did the witch say when she lost her broomstick key?

- "I guess I'll be *walking the spell-line* today!"

Why don't witches wear bowties?

- They prefer their magic a little *untied*.

What's a witch's favorite holiday outfit?

- Her *hex-tra special* robe!

What kind of socks do witches wear?

- *Broom-stitch* socks, of course!

Why did the witch refuse to wear jeans?

- She said, "These just aren't *spell-astic* enough for me!"

What's a witch's favorite fabric?

- *Spell-icate* silk!

Why do witches love dressing up?

- Because they're always in the mood for *spell-binding* fashion!

With all these jokes about a witch's wardrobe, one thing's for sure: witches have some seriously magical style! Whether it's their pointy hats or their flowing robes, their fashion choices are as enchanting as their spells!

Spooky School Days

itch school is a place full of bubbling cauldrons, enchanted textbooks, and some very magical mischief! From potion-making disasters to broomstick flying lessons, every day at spooky school is an adventure. Let's dive into the funniest happenings at witch school, where the students and teachers never fail to cast a spell of laughter!

Why did the witch fail potion class?
- She couldn't *stir* up enough enthusiasm!

What did the witch say when she dropped her potion book?
- "Looks like I'll need a *spell-check*!"

Why was the witch always late to broom-flying class?
- Because she kept getting *swept away* by her other lessons!

What's a witch's favorite subject in school?
- *Spelling*, of course!

Why did the witch bring a ladder to her magic exam?

- She wanted to *climb* her way to the top of the class!

Why was the witch's report card covered in glitter?

- Because she used a *sparkle* spell to make her grades look better!

What's a witch's favorite class project?

- Making a *brew-print* for her next potion!

Why did the witch fail her cauldron test?

- She couldn't *boil* down the important points!

Why did the witch's potion turn green?

- Because she added a little too much *spell-ach*!

What do witches eat for lunch at school?

- *Sand-witches*, of course!

Why did the witch bring a broomstick to her math test?

- To help her *sweep* through all the questions!

What's a witch's least favorite subject?

- *History*—because it's all about things that have already *passed*!

What happened when the witch cast a spell on her math homework?

- It became an *absolute mess-timate*!

Why did the witch's teacher send her home?

- She kept making *trouble brew*!

Why did the witch sit in the back of the classroom?

- So she could keep an *eye of newt* on everyone!

What did the witch write in her homework?

- "This is a real *cauldron-undrum*!"

What's a witch's favorite sport in gym class?

- *Broom-stickball*!

Why did the witch fail her flying test?

- She kept getting *grounded*!

What did the teacher say when the witch mixed up all the potions?

- "Now this is what I call a *potion-ate* disaster!"

Why do witches love science class?

- Because they get to do *experi-mints* with spells!

Why did the witch's spellbook fall apart?

- She didn't use enough *binding* magic!

What did the witch say when her spell didn't work?

- "Looks like I need to go back to *witch school*!"

Why did the witch get in trouble during history class?

- She kept trying to *rewrite* history with her spells!

What did the witch do when she couldn't find her broomstick in class?

- She said, "I guess I'll just have to *wing* it today!"

Why was the witch's report card covered in smoke?

- Because she *burned* through her studies!

Why did the witch teacher always bring a cauldron to class?

- To keep the students' attention *boiling*!

Why did the witch use a crystal ball during her math test?

- To help her *predict* the right answers!

Why do witches always pass music class?

- They're great at casting a *spell* of harmony!

What's a witch's favorite instrument?

- The *spella-phone*!

Why did the witch sit next to the cauldron during lunch?

- So she could *stir* up some conversation!

Why did the witch love art class?

- She got to draw *magic circles* all day!

What did the witch say when her spellbook disappeared?

- "That's a real *vanishing* act!"

Why did the witch get sent to detention?

- She kept casting *interrupting* spells!

What happened when the witch brought her pet cat to school?

- The teacher said, "No *purr-sonal pets* allowed!"

Why was the witch's locker always so messy?

- She couldn't stop *brewing up* trouble inside it!

What did the witch say when her magic broom didn't fly?

- "I guess I need to *brush up* on my skills!"

Why did the witch love recess?

- It gave her time to *re-charge* her magic!

What's a witch's favorite snack during school?

- *Spell-berry pie*!

Why did the witch's school uniform turn into a rainbow?

- She accidentally cast a *color-changing* spell on it!

What did the witch say when she aced her potion test?

- "I really *stirred* up some success this time!"

What did the teacher say when the witch mixed up all the ingredients in class?

- "That's a real *potion commotion*!"

Why do witches get along with math teachers?

- Because they know how to handle *fractions*—especially when dividing their magic potions!

Why was the witch's backpack so heavy?

- She filled it with too many *spell books*!

What's a witch's least favorite thing to do at school?

- *Homework*—because it's already *work* and it's at *home*!

Why did the witch always raise her hand in class?

- So she could cast a *volunteer* spell to answer questions!

What did the witch teacher say during broomstick flying lessons?

- "Make sure you don't get *swept away* by the excitement!"

Why did the witch bring a cauldron to lunch?

- She wanted to brew up some *conversation* with her classmates!

Why do witches love field trips?

- It's the perfect time for some *out-of-class magic*!

What did the witch say when she got a perfect score on her flying test?

- "I'm flying *high* now!"

Why was the witch's classroom so spooky?

- Because it was full of *spell-books and broomsticks*!

What's a witch's favorite part of science class?

- Making *potion* explosions!

Why did the witch giggle during broomstick flying lessons?

- She couldn't stop thinking about *sweeping* away the competition!

What happened when the witch cast a spell on her teacher?

- The teacher gave her extra *spellwork* for homework!

And that's all the fun for **Spooky School Days**! Whether it's potion classes gone wrong or broomstick flying lessons that don't go as planned, witch school is full of magical mishaps and lots of laughs!

Magical Pets

Witches are known for their magical companions, from black cats to toads and even talking ravens. These pets aren't your ordinary animals—they've got magic, attitude, and sometimes a little mischief. Let's have some fun with the silliest, most magical pet jokes in the witching world!

What's a witch's favorite animal?

- A *spelly-fish*!

Why did the witch's cat refuse to do magic?

- He said he was *purr-plexed* by all the spells!

What do you call a frog that hangs out with a witch?

- A *ribbit*-ing friend!

Why did the witch adopt a toad?

- Because he was always willing to *hop* in and help with her potions!

What's a witch's favorite type of bird?

- A *spell-crow*!

Why do witches love owls?

- Because they're so *hoot-dini*—they always disappear when you need them!

Why did the witch's black cat sit on her broomstick?

- To make sure he didn't get *swept* away!

What's a witch's snake called?

- A *hiss-terious* pet!

Why did the witch bring her parrot to class?

- So he could *spell* all the answers for her!

What do you get when you mix a witch and a rabbit?

- A *hare*-raising adventure!

Why did the witch's bat refuse to fly?

- He said he was afraid of getting *bat-tled* by the wind!

What's a witch's frog's favorite game?

- *Hopscotch*—with a dash of magic!

What did the witch's raven say when he forgot the spell?

- "Never-*moor* spells for me!"

Why did the witch name her pet snake "Hiss-teria"?

- Because he was always causing *hiss-terical* trouble!

Why don't witches bring fish to broomstick races?

- Because they always get *out of their depth*!

What's a witch's cat's favorite spell?

- *Purr-sonify*—he always wants to be treated like a human!

Why did the witch's owl never tell jokes?

- He was afraid he'd be too much of a *hoot*!

What's a witch's dog's favorite trick?

- *Abracadabra-fetch!* He always fetches with a little bit of magic!

What happened when the witch tried to teach her cat magic?

- He said, "I'll *purr-actice* later!"

Why did the witch's toad always follow her around?

- Because he was *toad-ally* in awe of her spells!

What do you call a witch with a magical hamster?

- A *spell-wheel* expert!

Why do witches love having bats as pets?

- Because they're always *hanging out* in the best places!

Why did the witch's crow never share his secrets?

- Because he was always *raven*-ous for attention!

What's a witch's dog's favorite magic trick?

- *Sit-stay-presto!* He can disappear from one spot and appear in another!

Why did the witch's snake always win at charades?

- Because he was great at *hiss-pering* clues!

What do witches call their mischievous cats?

- *Fur-tive* spell companions!

What did the witch's raven say when he lost a feather?

- "That's *un-feather-tunate*!"

Why did the witch's frog always carry a suitcase?

- Because he was ready to *hop* into action at any moment!

What's a witch's rabbit's favorite spell?

- The *hare-raising* one—it makes him jump!

Why did the witch's cat sit on top of the cauldron?

- Because he wanted to keep things *brewing* with excitement!

Why don't witches ever bring a rooster to their coven?

- Because he keeps *cock-a-doodling* the wrong spells!

What happened when the witch's toad drank the wrong potion?

- He became *hopping* mad!

Why do witches' snakes love libraries?

- Because they love reading *hiss-stories*!

What's a witch's favorite sea creature?

- A *spell-fish*—because it can swim through spells!

Why did the witch's dog refuse to chase his tail?

- He said he was too *spell-bound* to move!

What did the witch's cat say when he finally learned a spell?

- "*Fur-get* about it—I'm a natural!"

Why do witches love having rats as pets?

- Because they're always *scurrying* to help with spells!

What do you call a frog that helps a witch make potions?

- A *toad-al* genius!

Why did the witch's bat hang upside down during class?

- Because he wanted to *flip* through the spellbook!

What did the witch say to her pet pig?

- "You're such a little *pig-sus*, always flying into my spells!"

Why do witches have so many magical pets?

- Because they're all *spell-binding* company!

What did the witch's snake say when he got tangled up?

- "I'm a little *tied up* in magic right now!"

Why did the witch's cat refuse to ride on the broomstick?

- He said he was afraid of getting *swept* up in the action!

Why do witches love frogs?

- Because they always have a *hoppy* attitude!

What do you call a witch's bat that can do magic tricks?

- A real *winged-wonder*!

Why did the witch's dog always carry a broomstick?

- He was *swept* away by all the fun!

What's a witch's favorite thing to say to her owl?

- "You're a real *hoot*!"

Why do witches' frogs always make the best brews?

- Because they know how to *hop right in*!

What happened when the witch's parrot learned a spell?

- He couldn't stop *squawking* about it!

Why did the witch's raven always bring shiny things to class?

- Because he liked to keep his spells *bright*!

Why did the witch's hamster keep running in his wheel?

- He was working on a *round-the-clock* spell!

What do you call a witch's fish with magical powers?

- An *enchanting* swimmer!

Why did the witch's pet rat refuse to sit still?

- Because he was always *squeaking* out of trouble!

Why did the witch bring her bat to the party?

- Because he was a *wingman*!

What's a witch's favorite type of lizard?

- A *gecko*—because it sticks to magic!

Why did the witch's crow never miss a class?

- He was always looking to *raven-ge* his grades!

Why did the witch name her cat "Whiskers the Wizard"?

- Because he always had a *purr-fect* spell up his sleeve!

Witches in the Kitchen

In a witch's kitchen, you'll find more than just recipes—there's a cauldron full of potions, enchanted ingredients, and lots of magical cooking mishaps! Let's stir up some laughter with these jokes about witches and their unique way of whipping up tasty (or sometimes spooky) treats!

What does a witch serve for breakfast?
- *Poach-ed eggs* with a dash of spell!

Why did the witch bring her cauldron to the café?
- She wanted to brew up some *java-spresso*!

What's a witch's favorite thing to cook for dinner?
- *Spaghetti spells*—it's always tangled in magic!

Why don't witches ever order takeout?
- Because they prefer *stirring* up their own meals!

What did the witch say when her potion overflowed?
- "That's a real *brew-saster*!"

What do witches eat for dessert?

- *Spell-cakes* with a side of *hex-cream*!

Why did the witch's stew taste funny?

- She accidentally added a pinch of *laughing powder*!

What's a witch's favorite kitchen tool?

- Her *spell-ting* spoon, of course!

Why did the witch's potion turn bright pink?

- She mixed in some *giggle berries*!

What do witches serve at their tea parties?

- *Witch-brewed* tea and *enchanted scones*!

Why did the witch fail cooking class?

- Because she couldn't stop *spelling* out the wrong ingredients!

What's a witch's favorite snack?

- *Broomsticks* with a side of magical hummus!

Why did the witch bring a broom to her cooking lesson?

- She wanted to *sweep* through her recipes quickly!

What did the witch say when her cake collapsed?

- "Looks like I'll have to *spell* it back together!"

What do you call a witch who can't cook?

- A real *spell-mess* in the kitchen!

Why did the witch's pie taste so bad?

- She forgot to add the *magic touch*!

What's a witch's least favorite thing to bake?

- *Muffin spells*—because they never rise right!

What did the witch say when her bread didn't rise?

- "I guess it needs a little more *spell flour*!"

Why do witches love baking cakes?

- Because they get to put a little *magic* in every slice!

What did the witch do when her potion turned blue?

- She said, "I guess I'll make some *blueberry spells*!"

Why did the witch throw out her old cauldron?

- It couldn't *handle* the heat anymore!

What do witches use to spice up their potions?

- A sprinkle of *giggle dust* and a dash of *hex-a-pepper*!

Why did the witch's cookies disappear?

- They were *vanishing spell* cookies!

What's a witch's favorite soup?

- *Cauldron-der* soup with a side of enchanted breadsticks!

Why did the witch put her broom in the oven?

- She wanted to bake a *sweep-treat*!

What do witches use to measure their ingredients?

- *Spell-cups*—they hold exactly one magical portion!

What did the witch say when her soup turned green?

- "It's a little too *potion-y* for my taste!"

Why did the witch's stew bubble over?

- She put in too much *boiling giggles*!

What's a witch's favorite recipe?

- A *spell-mixed* salad with enchanted dressing!

Why do witches always stir their potions clockwise?

- Because it helps the *magic rise* to the top!

What do witches put on their sandwiches?

- A slice of *hex-cheese* with a sprinkle of spell salt!

Why did the witch add glitter to her stew?

- She wanted to make it *sparkle* with flavor!

What's a witch's favorite ice cream flavor?

- *Vanilla spell-scream*!

Why did the witch's potion fizz out of control?

- She added too much *bubble-bewitchment*!

What does a witch call her favorite kitchen towel?

- Her *enchant-o-rag*—it cleans up all magical messes!

What's a witch's favorite type of sandwich?

- A *witch-wich* with a side of spell fries!

Why did the witch use her wand to chop vegetables?

- She was in a hurry and needed to *slice and dice* with magic!

What did the witch say when her cake batter bubbled?

- "Looks like I've got some *spell-icious* magic brewing in there!"

What's a witch's favorite candy?

- *Frog's legs* dipped in enchanted chocolate!

Why don't witches use microwaves?

- Because they prefer their food *slow-brewed* in the cauldron!

Why did the witch sprinkle frog legs in her soup?

- Because it's a *hoppy* recipe!

What do witches use instead of sugar?

- A spoonful of *fairy dust*—it's extra sweet!

Why do witches love making pancakes?

- Because they can flip them with a flick of the wand!

What's a witch's favorite thing to drink at breakfast?

- A tall glass of *spell-berry juice*!

Why did the witch's cookies come out flat?

- She forgot to *levitate* the dough!

What does a witch serve for lunch?

- *Broomstick* sandwiches and *witch chips*!

What happened when the witch added too much pepper to her stew?

- It caused a *sneeze spell* that echoed through the whole castle!

What's a witch's favorite seasoning?

- *Creepy cumin* with a dash of *ghostly garlic*!

Why did the witch's pumpkin pie glow?

- She used a *glowing spell* instead of cinnamon!

What do witches call their magical recipe books?

- *Spell-cipes* for success!

What do witches use to cut their vegetables?

- A *witchery knife*—it slices with a spell!

Why did the witch's potion turn into a cake?

- She mixed up her spells and ended up with a *magic bake*!

What do witches serve at barbecues?

- *Bat wings* and *frog leg burgers*!

What did the witch say when her cauldron started to boil over?

- "This is going to be a real *over-brew* situation!"

Why did the witch put mushrooms in her potion?

- Because she wanted it to be a little *spell-y* and magical!

What did the witch make for a snack?

- A *spell-tacular* smoothie with batwing sprinkles!

Why did the witch's cake taste like magic?

- She added a sprinkle of *spell sugar* and a dash of *enchant-mint*!

What do witches use to grill their food?

- A *cauldron grill*—it adds a magical char to everything!

Why did the witch bake a cake for her broomstick?

- Because she wanted to make a *sweep-tastic* treat!

Broomstick Blunders

In the world of witches, broomsticks aren't just for sweeping floors—they're magical flying machines! But let's be honest, flying a broomstick isn't as easy as it looks. From mid-air mishaps to broom malfunctions, witches have their fair share of *sweep-tacular* blunders. So buckle up your broom belts and get ready for some high-flying laughs!

Why did the witch stop flying her broom?
- She swept too many people off their feet!

What happened when the witch's broom got a flat tire?
- She had to *sweep* it under the rug!

Why don't witches take their brooms to the mechanic?
- Because they always *fix* things with a spell!

What do you call a witch who's bad at flying her broom?
- A real *crash course* in magic!

Why did the witch's broom refuse to fly?

- It had a case of the *sweeps*!

What's a broomstick's favorite kind of music?

- *Sweep-hop*! It's got a great beat!

Why did the witch bring a mop to broom-flying class?

- She thought she could *clean up* the competition!

Why do witches have to be careful on their brooms during rush hour?

- Because they might get stuck in a *traffic jam*! (Especially if there's a full moon!)

What did the witch say when her broom ran out of magic mid-flight?

- "Looks like I'm about to *crash-land* into my next spell!"

Why don't witches play broomstick tag?

- Because the game always ends in a *sweep-stakes* disaster!

What did the witch do when her broom got stuck in a tree?

- She told it to *leaf* immediately!

Why did the witch's broomstick take a vacation?

- It needed some *down time* from all the flying!

What do witches do when their broomsticks won't start?

- They give them a good *kick-start* spell!

What's a witch's favorite type of race?

- The *broomstick 500*—no wheels, just pure magic!

Why did the witch get grounded from her broomstick?

- She kept *sweeping* in the wrong direction!

Why did the witch attach a GPS to her broomstick?

- So she wouldn't get *swept* away in the wrong direction!

What's a broomstick's favorite movie?

- *The Fast and the Sweep-erious*!

What did the witch say when her broomstick got a speeding ticket?

- "But officer, I was just *sweeping* through the clouds!"

Why do broomsticks always make terrible passengers?

- Because they hate being *swept* aside!

What did the witch do when she hit turbulence on her broom?

- She cast a *smooth-ride* spell and held on tight!

Why did the witch's broomstick get dizzy?

- It kept *spinning* out of control!

Why did the witch's broom have stage fright?

- It didn't want to *sweep* under the spotlight!

What do you call a broomstick that's always late?

- A real *sweep-slow*!

Why did the witch's broomstick keep flying in circles?

- It got caught in a *whirl-wind* of magic!

What happened when the witch's broomstick fell apart mid-flight?

- It was a real *sweep-cident*!

What's a broomstick's favorite exercise?

- *Sweeping squats*—gotta keep those broom handles strong!

Why did the witch take her broomstick to the doctor?

- Because it had a bad case of the *sweeps*!

Why don't broomsticks ever get tired?

- They've got *endless sweeping* power!

What did the witch say when her broomstick flew into a tree?

- "Well, that was *tree-mendous*!"

Why did the witch's broomstick quit its job?

- It felt *swept aside* by all the new magical gadgets!

What's a witch's broomstick's favorite dessert?

- *Sweep-tarts*!

Why did the witch's broomstick go on strike?

- It was tired of always being *swept off its feet*!

What happened when the witch forgot to recharge her broomstick?

- It became a real *snooze stick* mid-flight!

Why did the witch bring a spare broomstick to the party?

- Just in case things got *swept away* with fun!

What's a broomstick's favorite vacation spot?

- *Sweeping Sands* Beach, of course!

What did the witch say when her broomstick started to snore?

- "Looks like I need to *sweep-wake* it up!"

Why don't broomsticks enjoy roller coasters?

- They prefer a *smoother sweep* through the sky!

Why did the witch's broomstick need a nap?

- It had been *sweeping* around the clock!

What did the witch do when her broomstick broke down mid-flight?

- She called for a magical *broomstick-tow*!

Why did the witch's broomstick join the gym?

- To get in *sweep-tacular* shape!

What's a broomstick's favorite TV show?

- *Sweeping Through the Clouds*!

Why did the witch buy a broomstick with Wi-Fi?

- So she could stay *connected* while flying through the sky!

What did the witch say when her broomstick refused to move?

- "Looks like I'll need to *sweep* up a new one!"

Why did the witch decorate her broomstick with glitter?

- Because she wanted to make it *shine* while sweeping through the sky!

What do you call a witch's broomstick that tells jokes?

- A real *sweep-comedian*!

Why did the witch's broomstick get jealous of her cauldron?

- Because it wanted to be part of the *stir*ring action!

What did the witch say when her broomstick started talking back?

- "Hey, who put a *spell* on you?"

Why did the witch give her broomstick a day off?

- It had been working *sweep-stakes* too hard!

What's a broomstick's favorite holiday?

- *Sweeping-ween*!

Why don't broomsticks get along with vacuums?

- They feel *swept* under the rug by modern technology!

What happened when the witch's broomstick got tangled in a cloud?

- She had to *sweep* it out of trouble!

What's a broomstick's favorite subject in school?

- *Sweeping history*—it's been around for ages!

Why did the witch's broomstick fall asleep mid-flight?

- It had been flying *non-sweep* for hours!

What do you call a broomstick that's always telling spooky stories?

- A *sweep-tacular* storyteller!

What's a broomstick's favorite hobby?

- *Sweeping up* the competition at broom races!

Why did the witch's broomstick need glasses?

- It kept *sweeping* into things!

Why don't witches ever lose their broomsticks?

- Because they always keep them on a *short leash*—or a spell!

What did the witch do when her broomstick got tangled in the wind?

- She cast a *sweep-it-out* spell and kept on flying!

Why did the witch's broomstick start playing music?

- It wanted to be the next *sweep-erstar*!

What's a broomstick's favorite game?

- *Sweeping solitaire*—just one broom, one goal!

Spells Gone Wrong

E very witch knows that sometimes, even the best-laid spells can go completely off the rails! From potion explosions to invisible mishaps, there's no end to the magical mischief when spells don't go as planned. So, grab your wands, but be careful where you point them—things are about to get *spell-tastically* funny!

What happens when a witch's spell backfires?
- She gets a taste of her own *brew*!

Why did the witch's invisibility spell fail?
- Because she couldn't *see* where she went wrong!

What did the witch say when her spell accidentally turned her broom into a cactus?
- "Well, that was a *prickly* situation!"

Why don't witches use spellbooks from the library?
- Because the last one *disappeared* on them!

What did the witch do when her love spell went wrong?

- She accidentally made everyone fall in love with her *cat* instead!

Why did the witch's shrinking spell cause a big problem?

- It *blew up* in her face!

What did the witch say when her levitation spell failed?

- "I guess I'm *grounded* now!"

Why did the witch's potion explode?

- She added too much *fizz-a-ma-jig*!

What happened when the witch tried to turn her cat into a dragon?

- She ended up with a *fire-breathing* kitty instead!

Why did the witch cast a spell to turn herself into a rabbit?

- She wanted to have a *hopping* good time!

What did the witch do when she mixed up her memory spell?

- She forgot where she left her *wand*!

Why did the witch turn purple after casting a spell?

- She got her *spells crossed* and turned herself into a grape!

What happened when the witch tried to cast a sleep spell?

- She ended up putting her *broom* to sleep!

What did the witch say when her spellbook caught on fire?

- "Looks like I cast a little too much *firepower*!"

Why did the witch's hair turn green?

- Her beauty spell *backfired*!

What happens when a witch mixes a potion in a hurry?

- It causes a *spell-tastrophe*!

Why did the witch turn her cauldron into a bathtub?

- She got her *spells* all mixed up!

What did the witch say when her potion turned into jelly?

- "Well, this is a *wobble* of trouble!"

Why did the witch's invisibility spell wear off at the wrong time?

- She forgot to add the *vanish-vanilla*!

What did the witch do when she accidentally cast a spell on her shoes?

- They ran away without her!

Why did the witch's broomstick sprout wings?

- She used the wrong *flight* spell!

What happened when the witch cast a growth spell on her garden?

- The vegetables grew so big they turned into a *giant* problem!

Why did the witch's spell to make it rain backfire?

- She forgot to add the *rain-bow* ingredients!

What do you call a spell that turns everything upside down?

- A real *topsy-turvy* hex!

Why did the witch cast a spell to make her broomstick dance?

- She wanted a *sweep-stepping* partner!

What happened when the witch's transformation spell went wrong?

- She ended up with a *mouse* problem—literally!

Why did the witch accidentally turn her wand into spaghetti?

- She was trying to cook dinner with a little too much *magic*!

What did the witch do when she accidentally multiplied her broomsticks?

- She had a *sweeping* problem!

Why did the witch's spell make everyone laugh uncontrollably?

- She added too much *giggle root*!

What did the witch say when her spell turned everyone into frogs?

- "Looks like I've got a *ribbiting* situation on my hands!"

Why did the witch cast a spell on her socks?

- She wanted to give them a little *s-pair-it*!

What happened when the witch tried to teleport?

- She ended up in the *laundry room* instead of her magical tower!

Why did the witch's cauldron overflow with bubbles?

- She accidentally cast a *bubble bath* spell!

What did the witch do when her broomstick got stuck in a tree?

- She cast a *leaf-it-alone* spell and tried again!

Why did the witch turn herself into a squirrel?

- She wanted to *store* her magic for the winter!

What happened when the witch tried to cast a love spell on her crush?

- She accidentally made them fall in love with a *pumpkin*!

Why did the witch's spell make all her furniture float?

- She added a little too much *levitate leaf*!

What did the witch do when her talking spell went wrong?

- Her broom wouldn't stop *talking* back to her!

Why did the witch's mirror turn into a portal?

- She said, "Mirror, mirror, on the wall, let's go to the *mall*!"

What happened when the witch added fireworks to her spell?

- She created a *spark-tacular* disaster!

Why did the witch's frog start singing?

- She cast a *musical toad* spell by mistake!

What did the witch say when her spell made her house disappear?

- "I guess I really *vanished* into thin air this time!"

Why did the witch's hair start glowing?

- She mixed up her *shine-a-lot* spell with her invisibility potion!

What did the witch do when her broomstick multiplied by ten?

- She said, "I guess I'm going to have to *sweep* things up!"

Why did the witch's spell make her shoes turn into cupcakes?

- She added a little too much *sugar* to the mix!

Why did the witch's potion turn into a rainbow?

- She mixed in some *unicorn tears* by accident!

What happened when the witch tried to turn herself into a bat?

- She ended up as a *bathtub* instead!

Why did the witch's broomstick keep bouncing?

- She used the wrong *jumping spell*!

What did the witch say when her wand started dancing?

- "Looks like I've got a case of *wand-erlust*!"

Why did the witch's potion explode with glitter?

- She added too much *sparkle root*!

What happened when the witch tried to cast a freeze spell?

- Her potion turned into *ice cream*!

What did the witch say when her invisibility cloak stopped working?

- "Well, this is *cloak-tastrophe*!"

Why did the witch's cauldron start singing?

- She mixed up her *melody leaf* with her parsley!

What happened when the witch tried to make her bed with a spell?

- She accidentally turned it into a *water bed*!

Witchy Friends

Witch friendships are filled with fun, laughter, and a little bit of magic! Whether they're brewing potions together, going on broomstick adventures, or casting group spells, witch friends know how to make every day *magical*. But like any group of friends, things can get a little out of hand when too many spells get involved! Get ready for some enchanted laughs with these witchy friendship jokes.

Why did the witch's friends stop inviting her over?

- She was always *casting* a spell on the fun!

What's a witch coven's favorite group activity?

- A *potion party*—where everyone brews something special!

Why do witch friends always get along?

- They know how to *spell things out* for each other!

What did the witch say when her friend's potion went wrong?

- "Don't worry, we're in this *brew* together!"

Why did the witches argue over a broomstick?

- They couldn't decide who had *sweeping* rights!

What do witch friends do when they hang out?

- They have a *spook-tacular* time casting spells and laughing!

Why did the witch's best friend always bring extra wands?

- Just in case they needed to *cast* some extra fun!

Why don't witch friends ever argue for long?

- Because they're always willing to *patch things up* with a little magic!

What's a witch's favorite game to play with friends?

- *Hex-and-seek*—but watch out for disappearing spells!

Why did the witches get in trouble during group spell practice?

- They created a *potion explosion* that covered the entire room in glitter!

What do witches call their group chat?

- The *Spell-Casters Club*!

Why did the witch's friend always bring her own cauldron?

- She didn't want to *stir up* any trouble!

Why did the witches have a bake-off?

- To see who could make the most *spell-tacular* cake!

What's a witch's favorite sleepover activity?

- Casting *dream spells* and staying up all night laughing!

Why did the witch's friend bring a broom to their picnic?

- To help *sweep away* any ants that tried to crash the party!

What did the witch say to her friend after a long broomstick ride?

- "We've been flying *high* all day!"

Why did the witches have a potion-making competition?

- To see who could *brew* the most magical drink!

What's a witch coven's favorite holiday?

- *Witchmas*—where they exchange enchanted gifts!

Why did the witch's friends cast a spell on her broomstick?

- They wanted to give her a *boost* to make her fly faster!

What do you call a group of witches who love to travel together?

- The *Wander-Covens*—always flying off on new adventures!

Why did the witch's friend wear a helmet on her broomstick ride?

- She didn't want to *crash* the fun!

Why do witches never let their friends cast spells alone?

- Because casting spells together is way more *spell-tacular*!

What did the witch say when her friend's spell turned the sky green?

- "Now that's what I call a *colorful* friendship!"

Why did the witch's coven meet every full moon?

- To *shine* some light on their next magical adventure!

What's a witch's favorite thing to do with her friends?

- Brew up some laughs and *stir* things up with magic!

Why did the witches start a band?

- They wanted to create some *spell-binding* music together!

What do witch friends call their group spells?

- *Witch-tastic collaborations*!

Why did the witches get lost on their way to the magic forest?

- Their *broomstick GPS* wasn't working!

What do you call a group of witches who love to dance?

- The *Broom-Boogie Coven*!

Why did the witches make matching cloaks?

- So they could all look *spell-tacular* together!

What did the witch say when her friend cast a rain spell during their picnic?

- "Well, this is a *wet* situation!"

Why did the witches decorate their cauldrons with glitter?

- To add a little *sparkle* to their potions!

What do witches do when they have a disagreement?

- They have a *spell-off* to see who can cast the funniest spell!

Why did the witch bring extra wands to the party?

- In case anyone needed a *backup spell* for fun!

What do witches do when they're not casting spells?

- They're usually *cackling* with laughter!

Why did the witches have a broomstick race?

- To see who could *sweep* the competition away!

What do witch friends give each other for birthdays?

- A new *enchanted wand* to cast even more fun spells!

Why did the witches throw a party at the haunted house?

- Because they knew it would be a *spook-tacular* time!

What's a witch's favorite way to communicate with friends?

- *Broom-mail*—delivered right to your cauldron!

Why did the witches have a potion-making sleepover?

- So they could *brew* up some laughs together all night long!

What did the witch say when her friend cast a spell that made her float?

- "Well, this friendship is really *lifting* me up!"

Why did the witches go on a road trip?

- They needed a break from flying on broomsticks—time for a *spell-tacular* adventure on the ground!

What do witches call their secret handshakes?

- *Hex-shakes*—you can't leave a coven meeting without one!

Why did the witch's friends surprise her with a new broom-stick?

- To help her *fly high* in style!

What do witches do when they all wear the same hat?

- They call it a *witchy coincidence*!

Why did the witches take turns casting spells?

- To make sure everyone got a chance to *brew* up some fun!

What's a witch's favorite group exercise?

- *Broomstick aerobics*—it's a real workout!

Why did the witches have a cauldron-decorating contest?

- To see who could make the most *spell-tacular* cauldron!

What did the witch say when her friend accidentally turned her into a frog?

- "Looks like we'll need to *ribbit* back to normal!"

Why did the witches start a spell-casting club?

- So they could *cast spells* and *cast laughs* all day long!

What do witches call their group photo?

- A *coven snapshot*—always with enchanted smiles!

Why did the witches host a broomstick fashion show?

- To show off their *spell-binding* new rides!

What's a witch's favorite thing to do at a slumber party?

- Cast *dreamy spells* and stay up talking all night!

Halloween Hijinks

Halloween is the witchiest night of the year! From trick-or-treating to spooky pranks, witches have a blast getting into the Halloween spirit—sometimes a little *too* much fun. Whether they're handing out enchanted candy or pulling magical pranks, witches make Halloween extra spooky and silly. Get ready for some Halloween hijinks with these ghoulishly funny jokes!

What do witches hand out on Halloween?

- *Boo-berry* pie!

Why did the witch refuse to wear a costume on Halloween?

- She said, "I'm already dressed as a *professional witch*!"

What's a witch's favorite Halloween treat?

- *Spell-tacular* candy corn!

Why did the witch bring a cauldron to the Halloween party?

- She wanted to *brew up* some fun!

What do witches give out instead of candy?

- *Hexed lollipops* that disappear after one lick!

Why did the witch's pumpkin start glowing?

- She cast a *light-up* spell for Halloween!

What's a witch's favorite Halloween decoration?

- *Flying broomsticks*—they're a real *sweeping* success!

Why did the witch's Halloween costume disappear?

- She accidentally cast an invisibility spell on it!

What do witches do when they run out of candy on Halloween?

- They make *magic treats* with a flick of their wand!

Why do witches love Halloween so much?

- It's the one night of the year they can go *broom-to-broom* with everyone else!

What did the witch say when she saw a jack-o'-lantern?

- "Nice face! But you're missing the *magic* glow."

What's a witch's favorite Halloween game?

- *Broomstick bowling*—you have to knock over the pumpkins with your broom!

Why did the witch's costume party get out of hand?

- Too many people tried casting *costume change* spells at the same time!

What's a witch's favorite Halloween song?

- *Ghostbusters*—because they always need a little *ghost control*!

Why did the witch's trick-or-treat bag start flying away?

- She accidentally enchanted it to *float* through the air!

What did the witch say when her broomstick got tangled in Halloween decorations?

- "Looks like we've got a *sweep-tacular* situation here!"

Why did the witch's candy turn green?

- She put in too much *frog juice* for flavor!

What do witches use to decorate their haunted houses?

- *Spooky cobwebs* and *glowing pumpkins*!

What's a witch's favorite thing to say while trick-or-treating?

- "*Trick or broom*—I'll take either!"

Why did the witch's cat get scared on Halloween?

- It saw its own *shadow* and thought it was a ghost!

What do witches drink at Halloween parties?

- *Witch's brew*-punch—it's magically delicious!

Why did the witch's pumpkin start dancing?

- She cast a *groovy gourd* spell on it!

What do witches do after trick-or-treating?

- They *sort* through their candy to find the most magical treats!

Why did the witch's cauldron overflow on Halloween?

- She added too much *candy corn* to her potion!

What did the witch say when her broomstick wouldn't fly on Halloween?

- "Looks like I'm *grounded* for the night!"

What's a witch's favorite spooky prank?

- *Vanishing candy*—it disappears just when you're about to eat it!

Why did the witch's hat start glowing?

- She enchanted it with a little *Halloween magic*!

What do witches wear to Halloween parties?

- Their *best robes* and *glow-in-the-dark hats*!

Why did the witch carve a pumpkin into a frog?

- She thought it would make a *ribbit-ing* jack-o'-lantern!

What do witches put in their Halloween punch?

- A little bit of *giggle potion* for laughs!

Why did the witch's broomstick keep running into trees on Halloween?

- It was trying to *trick or treat* with its own route!

What did the witch say when she pulled a prank on her friend?

- "Looks like you got *spell-tricked*!"

Why do witches love going to haunted houses?

- Because they get to practice their *spooking skills*!

What's a witch's favorite Halloween spell?

- *Candy-appearo*—it makes candy appear out of thin air!

Why did the witch bring a toad to the Halloween party?

- She wanted someone to *hop* the dance floor with!

What do witches call their Halloween potluck?

- A *cauldron cook-off*, with magical dishes!

Why did the witch's broomstick fly backward on Halloween?

- It got *spooked* by a ghost!

What did the witch say when her trick-or-treat bag vanished?

- "Guess I should've used a *no-vanish* spell!"

Why do witches go trick-or-treating with their cats?

- Because their cats know all the best *haunted houses*!

What's a witch's favorite thing to give out on Halloween?

- *Haunted lollipops* that glow in the dark!

Why did the witch cast a dance spell on Halloween?

- To turn the party into a *witching hour boogie*!

What do witches do when their pumpkins get too big?

- They cast a *shrinking spell*—who needs a giant jack-o'-lantern?

Why did the witch's hat keep flying off on Halloween?

- It wanted to *join the fun* in the sky!

What's a witch's favorite Halloween candy?

- *Bat-shaped chocolates* with a spellbinding crunch!

Why did the witch's spellbook start glowing on Halloween night?

- It was ready for some *spooky spellcasting*!

What do witches call their Halloween sleepover?

- A *haunted slumber party*—with lots of spooky fun!

Why did the witch's costume keep changing?

- She cast a *costume-flip* spell by accident!

What's a witch's favorite Halloween tradition?

- *Flying* over the trick-or-treaters to give them a spook!

Why did the witch's broomstick glow in the dark?

- She added a little *glitter spell* for extra shine!

What do witches call their Halloween pranks?

- *Hex-tacular* tricks that always end in laughter!

Why did the witch's broomstick get stuck in a pumpkin patch?

- It couldn't resist the *pumpkin magic* in the air!

What did the witch say when she scared all the trick-or-treaters?

- "I guess I put a little too much *boo* in my *spook*!"

What's a witch's favorite trick-or-treat strategy?

- *Fly-by candy collecting*—she swoops down and grabs the best treats!

Why did the witch's potion glow on Halloween night?

- She added a touch of *moonlight magic* for an extra spooky effect!

Potions and Brew-haha

In the magical world of witches, potion-making is both an art and a science—but sometimes it's also a recipe for laughter! Whether it's a potion bubbling over or a spell gone hilariously wrong, witches are always stirring up some trouble in their cauldrons. Get ready to brew up some fun with these potion-filled jokes!

Why did the witch bring a broom to the café?

- To *stir up* some trouble!

What happened when the witch's potion overflowed?

- It caused a real *brew-saster*!

Why don't witches use spoons in their potions?

- They prefer to *stir* things up with magic!

What do you call a potion that makes everyone laugh?

- A *giggle-brew*!

Why did the witch's potion turn green?

- She added too much *frog juice*!

What did the witch say when her potion started bubbling over?

- "Looks like I've brewed up a *cauldron catastrophe*!"

What do you get when a witch mixes a potion too quickly?

- A *spell-tacular mess*!

Why did the witch add sprinkles to her potion?

- She wanted it to look *spell-tacular*!

What did the witch do when her potion exploded?

- She said, "Well, that's one way to *stir* things up!"

Why did the witch's potion taste funny?

- She added too much *laughing powder*!

What do witches do when their potion bubbles too much?

- They call it a *bubble-trouble* brew!

Why did the witch's cauldron start glowing?

- She added a pinch of *star-dust* by accident!

What do witches drink in the morning?

- *Brewed coffee* with a side of magical mischief!

Why did the witch's potion turn into a rainbow?

- She added a dash of *unicorn sparkle*!

What do witches call a potion that never works?

- A *flop brew*—and it always needs a little more magic!

Why did the witch bring a fan to her potion class?

- To keep cool when the *brew* gets too hot!

What did the witch do when her potion turned into jelly?

- She said, "I guess it's a *wobble-brew* now!"

Why do witches love brewing potions?

- Because it's a great way to *stir* up some fun!

What did the witch say when her potion exploded with glitter?

- "Now this is what I call a *sparkle-brew*!"

Why did the witch add marshmallows to her potion?

- She wanted to make a *fluffy brew*—light as air!

What do witches do when their potion gets too fizzy?

- They give it a good *stir* and hope for the best!

Why did the witch's potion sing a song?

- She added too much *melody root*!

What happened when the witch tried to make a potion for flying?

- It caused her to *float* away without her broomstick!

What do witches add to their potions when they're feeling silly?

- A dash of *giggle weed*—it always adds a laugh!

Why did the witch's potion turn into ice cream?

- She mixed up her *freeze spell* with her potion recipe!

What did the witch do when her cauldron overflowed?

- She said, "I guess I *brewed* too much of a good thing!"

Why did the witch's potion bubble up with fireworks?

- She accidentally added *firework fizzle* instead of frog legs!

What do you call a potion that changes color?

- A real *chameleon brew*!

Why did the witch's potion turn into a tornado?

- She added too much *whirlwind spice*!

What did the witch do when her potion turned her cat into a rabbit?

- She said, "Well, that's a real *hopping brew* now!"

Why did the witch bring a broomstick to her potion party?

- She wanted to help *sweep* up the mess!

What do witches use to taste-test their potions?

- A *spell-spoon*—but just a tiny sip!

Why did the witch's potion sparkle in the moonlight?

- She added a pinch of *moon dust*!

What did the witch say when her potion turned her into a frog?

- "I guess it's a *ribbiting* experience!"

Why do witches always follow their potion recipes?

- Because if they don't, it could turn into a *potion explosion*!

What happened when the witch tried to make an invisibility potion?

- She couldn't find it once it was ready!

Why did the witch's potion start bubbling over?

- She added too much *bubbly beet*!

What do witches do when their cauldron is too small for a big potion?

- They cast a *growth spell* on the cauldron!

What's a witch's favorite snack to add to her potion?

- *Magic mushrooms*—they always give it a little *extra flavor*!

Why did the witch's potion start dancing?

- She added some *boogie root* to the brew!

What do witches call a potion that fizzes up like soda?

- A *bubbling brew-splosion*!

Why did the witch's cauldron fill up with balloons?

- She added too much *floaty spell* to her potion!

What do witches do when their potion goes wrong?

- They *stir* it up and try again!

Why did the witch's potion make everyone giggle?

- It was a *giggle brew*, full of laughing magic!

What did the witch say when her potion made her broomstick disappear?

- "Now I've really *swept* away all the fun!"

Why did the witch's cauldron start floating in the air?

- She put in too much *light-as-air leaf*!

What did the witch do when her potion turned everyone into rabbits?

- She said, "Now this is a *hopping brew*!"

Why did the witch's potion glow in the dark?

- She added a dash of *glow-brew powder*!

What do witches do when their potion doesn't taste right?

- They add a little *magic sugar* to sweeten it up!

Why did the witch's potion start bubbling over with popcorn?

- She accidentally added *popping corn* instead of bat wings!

What do witches call their super spicy potions?

- *Fire-brews*—they're too hot to handle!

Why did the witch bring a mop to her potion-making class?

- To *clean up* any magical messes!

What did the witch do when her potion made her levitate?

- She said, "I guess I'm *floating* on magic now!"

Why did the witch's potion change color every minute?

- She added too much *rainbow herb*!

Why did the witch's cauldron start singing a lullaby?

- She put in a bit too much *sleepy root*!

What do witches use to stir their potions?

- A *magic wand spoon*, of course!

Why did the witch's potion overflow with confetti?

- She was trying to make a *party brew*—and it worked!

What happened when the witch put dragon scales in her potion?

- It caused a real *dragon-brew-splosion*!

Why did the witch's potion make her sneeze?

- She accidentally added *sneeze-brew powder*!

Wickedly Funny Witches

Witches aren't just great at casting spells—they're great at casting laughs too! From flying broomsticks to magical mishaps, witches know how to make any moment wickedly funny. This chapter is a grand finale, bringing together the best witch jokes that will make you laugh, cackle, and maybe even cast a giggle spell or two. Get ready for some wickedly funny fun!

What do you call a witch's garage sale?
- A *spell out* event!

Why did the witch start her own bakery?
- Because she had the *recipe for success*—a little magic and a lot of cake!

What did the witch say when her broomstick broke down?
- "Guess I'm going to have to *sweep* this under the rug!"

Why do witches always carry a pencil?
- To write down their *spell-checks*!

What's a witch's favorite ride at the amusement park?

- The *broomstick roller-coaster*—it's a real *whirl* of fun!

Why did the witch open a magic school?

- She wanted to teach others how to *spell it out*!

What do witches eat for lunch?

- *Sand-witches*!

Why did the witch cast a spell on her shoes?

- So she could always *step into* a magical moment!

What did the witch say when her spell worked perfectly?

- "Now that's what I call a *spell-binding* success!"

What do witches do when they're bored?

- They *brew* up a little fun!

Why did the witch start a band?

- She wanted to make some *spell-tacular* music!

What do you call a witch who tells jokes?

- A real *spell comedian*!

What's a witch's favorite TV show?

- *Bewitched*—because it's all about casting spells and having fun!

Why do witches love jokes about cauldrons?

- Because they're always *bubbling* with laughter!

What did the witch say when she lost her broomstick?

- "Well, this situation *sweeps*!"

Why did the witch wear sunglasses?

- To keep her spells from *shining* too brightly!

What do witches call their favorite shoes?

- *Broomstick boots*—perfect for flying and fashion!

Why did the witch bring a map to her spell-casting class?

- So she wouldn't get *lost* in her magic!

What's a witch's favorite time of day?

- The *witching hour*—when all the fun happens!

Why did the witch open a restaurant?

- Because her potions tasted so good, they were *cauldron-ary* delights!

What did the witch say when her potion started glowing?

- "Looks like I've made a *light brew*!"

Why don't witches need alarm clocks?

- Their *spells* always wake them up right on time!

What do witches say when they're in a rush?

- "Time to *broom* it!"

Why did the witch open a library?

- So everyone could check out her *spellbinding* books!

What do you call a witch who loves to organize her spells?

- A real *neat spell-freak*!

Why did the witch's hair turn into snakes?

- She cast a *bad hair day* spell by accident!

What did the witch say when her spellbook vanished?

- "Well, that's a real *disappearing act*!"

What's a witch's favorite holiday?

- *Witchmas*—because it's filled with magical surprises!

Why did the witch wear two hats?

- In case she needed to do *double magic*!

What do witches wear on their feet when they're relaxing?

- *Spell slippers*—perfect for cozy nights with a good spellbook!

Why did the witch get lost on her way to the potion party?

- She forgot to *follow the magic trail*!

What do witches do when they forget their spells?

- They have a little *spell amnesia*—until they find their wand!

Why do witches love to laugh?

- Because it keeps their *magic strong*!

What's a witch's favorite movie?

- *The Wizard of Giggles*—filled with magical laughs!

Why did the witch start wearing a cape?

- Because she wanted to look *super magical*!

What do witches call a really funny spell?

- A *laughing hex*!

Why did the witch throw her wand into the cauldron?

- She wanted to *stir up* some extra magic!

What do witches use to send messages?

- *Spell-mail*—delivered right to your broomstick!

What did the witch say when her broomstick went on vacation?

- "Looks like I'll need to *fly solo* for a while!"

Why did the witch's potion explode with glitter?

- She added a pinch of *sparkle magic* for good luck!

What do witches love to do at midnight?

- Fly around and *cast moonlight spells*!

Why did the witch's mirror start talking?

- She cast a *chatty reflection* spell by accident!

What do witches do when their wands don't work?

- They give them a little *magical reboot*!

Why did the witch bring her broomstick to the dance?

- She wanted to show off her *sweep moves* on the dance floor!

What do witches call their favorite potion recipe?

- A *brew-berry special*—with just the right amount of magic!

Why did the witch's house glow at night?

- She used a little *moonlight magic* to brighten things up!

What's a witch's favorite way to relax?

- Sitting by the fire with a cup of *brew-tea*!

What do witches do when they need a break?

- They take a *magic rest* and let their spells recharge!

Why did the witch's cauldron start singing?

- She added too much *melody potion*!

What do witches wear to fancy parties?

- Their *most magical robes*—with extra sparkle!

Why did the witch's potion turn into candy?

- She was trying to create a sweet spell and got a little carried away!

What do witches do when their broomsticks stop working?

- They take them in for a little *broom maintenance*!

Why do witches love Halloween?

- Because it's the one night they can show off their *spell-tacular* skills!

What do witches do when they want to share a joke?

- They cast a *laughing spell* and spread the giggles around!

What's a witch's favorite part of flying?

- *Sweeping* through the clouds with the wind in their hat!

Why did the witch's spell make everyone giggle?

- It was a *laughing potion*—and it worked too well!

What did the witch say when her broomstick ran out of magic?

- "Time to give it a *magic recharge*!"

What do witches call a really good joke?

- A *spell-tacular* laugh that's sure to fly!

Casting the Final Laugh

W ell, you've brewed your way through all the jokes, cackled with witches, and survived broomstick blunders! If your sides aren't sore from laughing and your cauldron hasn't bubbled over with giggles, then you're clearly ready for the next level of witchy comedy. Remember, the next time a spell goes wrong or a potion fizzes over, just laugh it off—after all, even witches need a good joke every now and then! Thanks for flying through this magical adventure with us, and don't forget to cast a spell for more laughter in the future. Now, go forth and spread those giggles like confetti from a cauldron!